July/Julio

By/Por Robyn Brode

Reading Consultant/Consultora de lectura: Linda Cornwell,
Literacy Connections Consulting/consultora de lectoescritura

WEEKLY READER®
PUBLISHING

Please visit our web site at **www.garethstevens.com**.
For a free catalog describing our list of high-quality books, call 1-800-542-2595 (USA)
or 1-800-387-3178 (Canada). Our fax: 1-877-542-2596

Library of Congress Cataloging-in-Publication Data
Brode, Robyn.
 [July. Spanish & English]
 July / by Robyn Brode ; reading consultant, Linda Cornwell — Julio / por Robyn Brode ;
 consultora de lectura, Linda Cornwell
  p. cm. — (Months of the year — Meses del año)
 English and Spanish in parallel text.
 Includes bibliographical references and index.
 ISBN-10: 1-4339-1935-4   ISBN-13: 978-1-4339-1935-0 (lib. bdg.)
 ISBN-10: 1-4339-2112-X   ISBN-13: 978-1-4339-2112-4 (softcover)
  1. July—Juvenile literature.   2. Holidays—United States—Juvenile literature.
 3. Vacations—United States—Juvenile literature.   I. Cornwell, Linda.   II. Title.   III. Title: Julio.
 GT4803.B6718   2010
 394.263—dc22   2009013984

This edition first published in 2010 by
Weekly Reader® Books
An Imprint of Gareth Stevens Publishing
1 Reader's Digest Road
Pleasantville, NY 10570-7000 USA

Copyright © 2010 by Gareth Stevens, Inc.

Executive Managing Editor: Lisa M. Herrington
Senior Editors: Barbara Bakowski, Jennifer Magid-Schiller
Designer: Jennifer Ryder-Talbot
Translators: Tatiana Acosta and Guillermo Gutiérrez

Photo Credits: Cover, back cover, title, pp. 9, 11, 15 © Ariel Skelley/Weekly Reader; p. 7 © C Squared
Studios/Getty Images; p. 13 © Morgan Lane Photography/Shutterstock; p. 17 © Suzanne Tucker/
Shutterstock; p. 19 © Ricardo Manuel Silva de Sousa/Shutterstock; p. 21 © Sonya Etchison/Shutterstock

Printed in the United States of America

1 2 3 4 5 6 7 8 9 10 11 10 09

Table of Contents/Contenido

Boldface words appear in the glossary.

Las palabras en **negrita** aparecen en el glosario.

Welcome to July!

July is the seventh month of the year.
July has 31 days. It is a **summer** month.

- - - - - - - - - -

¡Bienvenidos a julio!

Julio es el séptimo mes del año.
Julio tiene 31 días y es uno de los
meses del **verano**.

Months of the Year/Meses del año

Month/Mes	Number of Days/ Días en el mes
1 January/Enero	31
2 February/Febrero	28 or 29*/28 ó 29*
3 March/Marzo	31
4 April/Abril	30
5 May/Mayo	31
6 June/Junio	30
7 July/Julio	31
8 August/Agosto	31
9 September/Septiembre	30
10 October/Octubre	31
11 November/Noviembre	30
12 December/Diciembre	31

*February has an extra day every fourth year./Febrero tiene un día extra cada cuatro años.

In some places, July is very hot! When people are hot and thirsty, they enjoy a glass of cool **lemonade**.

- - - - - - - - - -

En algunos lugares, el mes de julio es muy caluroso. Cuando tenemos sed y calor, nos sienta bien un vaso de **limonada** fría.

lemonade/
limonada

25¢
LEMONADE

Summer Fun

Many people love to eat ice cream on hot days.

- - - - - - - - - -

Diversión de verano

A mucha gente le gusta comer helado los días que hace calor.

 What is your favorite flavor of ice cream?

- - - - - - -

¿Cuál es tu helado favorito?

In hot weather, kids have fun cooling off in a **sprinkler**.

‒ ‒ ‒ ‒ ‒ ‒ ‒ ‒ ‒

Cuando hace calor, los niños se refrescan jugando cerca de un **aspersor**.

 What is your favorite way to cool off?
‒ ‒ ‒ ‒ ‒ ‒ ‒
¿Qué te gusta hacer para refrescarte?

sprinkler/
aspersor

In summer, many kids go to camp. They swim, play games, and make new friends.

－ － － － － － － － －

En verano, muchos niños van a campamentos. Allí nadan, juegan y hacen amigos.

Happy Birthday, U.S.A.!

July 4 is **Independence Day**. This holiday is also called the Fourth of July. It celebrates the day when the United States of America became a country.

- - - - - - - - - -

¡Feliz cumpleaños, Estados Unidos!

En julio se celebra el **Día de la Independencia**. Esta fiesta también se conoce como el Cuatro de Julio. En esa fecha conmemoramos el día en que Estados Unidos se convirtió en una nación.

One way to celebrate the Fourth of July is to have a picnic. Juicy watermelon is a sweet summer treat!

— — — — — — — — —

Para celebrar el Cuatro de Julio, podemos hacer un picnic. ¡Un jugoso trozo de sandía dulce es uno de los placeres del verano!

**watermelon/
sandía**

17

On the Fourth of July, many people watch **fireworks**. The fireworks make loud popping noises as they light up the night sky. Boom!

- - - - - - - - - -

A muchos les gusta ver los **fuegos artificiales** del Cuatro de Julio. Los fuegos artificiales estallan ruidosamente e iluminan el cielo nocturno. ¡Pum!

fireworks/
fuegos artificiales

When July ends, it is time for August
to begin.

- - - - - - - - - -

Cuando julio termina, empieza agosto.

Glossary/Glosario

fireworks: a display of colored lights, smoke, and loud noise

Independence Day: July 4, a holiday that celebrates the day the United States became a country. It is also known as the Fourth of July.

lemonade: a drink made with lemon juice, water, sugar, and ice

sprinkler: a device that attaches to a hose. It has tiny holes to spray drops of water.

summer: the season between spring and fall, when the weather is the warmest of the year

- - - - - - - - -

aspersor: aparato que se conecta a una manguera y que tiene pequeños agujeros por los que sale agua a presión

Día de la Independencia: 4 de julio, fiesta en la que se celebra el día en que nació Estados Unidos. También se conoce como el Cuatro de Julio.

fuegos artificiales: exhibición de explosivos que producen luces de colores, humo y ruido

limonada: bebida que se hace con jugo de limón, agua, azúcar y hielo

verano: la estación del año entre la primavera y el otoño. Es la época más calurosa del año.

For More Information/Más información

Books/Libros

Fourth of July/Cuatro de julio. Our Country's Holidays/Las fiestas de nuestra nación (series). Sheri Dean (Gareth Stevens Publishing, 2006)

Summer/Verano. Seasons of the Year/Las estaciones del año (series). JoAnn Early Macken (Gareth Stevens Publishing, 2006)

Web Sites/Páginas web

Funschool Fun Blaster: Summer/Verano
funschool.kaboose.com/fun-blaster/summer
Find puzzles, coloring pages, games, and a quiz./Encuentren rompecabezas, páginas para colorear, juegos y una prueba.

KidsSoup: Fourth of July/Cuatro de Julio
www.kidssoup.com/4thofJuly/4thofJuly.html
Learn about the American flag, and make Fourth of July crafts./ Encuentren información sobre la bandera de Estados Unidos y hagan manualidades relacionadas con el Cuatro de Julio.

Index/Índice

About the Author

Robyn Brode has been a teacher, a writer, and an editor in the book publishing field for many years. She earned a bachelor's degree in English literature from the University of California, Berkeley.

Información sobre la autora

Robyn Brode ha sido maestra, escritora y editora de libros durante muchos años. Obtuvo su licenciatura en literatura inglesa en la Universidad de California, Berkeley.